STEAM JOBS IN

CYBER-SECURITY

Cynthia Argentine

ROURKE
Educational Media

A Division of
Carson Dellosa
Education

rourkeeducationalmedia.com

ROURKE'S
SCHOOL to HOME
CONNECTIONS
BEFORE AND DURING READING ACTIVITIES

Before Reading: *Building Background Knowledge and Vocabulary*

Building background knowledge can help children process new information and build upon what they already know. Before reading a book, it is important to tap into what children already know about the topic. This will help them develop their vocabulary and increase their reading comprehension.

Questions and Activities to Build Background Knowledge:

1. Look at the front cover of the book and read the title. What do you think this book will be about?
2. What do you already know about this topic?
3. Take a book walk and skim the pages. Look at the table of contents, photographs, captions, and bold words. Did these text features give you any information or predictions about what you will read in this book?

Vocabulary: *Vocabulary Is Key to Reading Comprehension*

Use the following directions to prompt a conversation about each word.

- Read the vocabulary words.
- What comes to mind when you see each word?
- What do you think each word means?

Vocabulary Words:
- bypassing
- encryption
- espionage
- exploit
- fraudulent
- legitimate
- lucrative
- personnel
- ransom
- router

During Reading: *Reading for Meaning and Understanding*

To achieve deep comprehension of a book, children are encouraged to use close reading strategies. During reading, it is important to have children stop and make connections. These connections result in deeper analysis and understanding of a book.

Close Reading a Text

During reading, have children stop and talk about the following:

- Any confusing parts
- Any unknown words
- Text to text, text to self, text to world connections
- The main idea in each chapter or heading

Encourage children to use context clues to determine the meaning of any unknown words. These strategies will help children learn to analyze the text more thoroughly as they read.

When you are finished reading this book, turn to the next-to-last page for **Text-Dependent Questions** and an **Extension Activity**.

TABLE OF CONTENTS

THE MANY FACES OF CYBERSECURITY

Late at night, a cyber-incident responder watches a computer screen. He sees unusual activity on his company's network. Immediately, he begins isolating the threat.

Across the country, a penetration tester attempts to hack into her company's network. She reports the weaknesses she finds. Her job is to beat illegal hackers at their game.

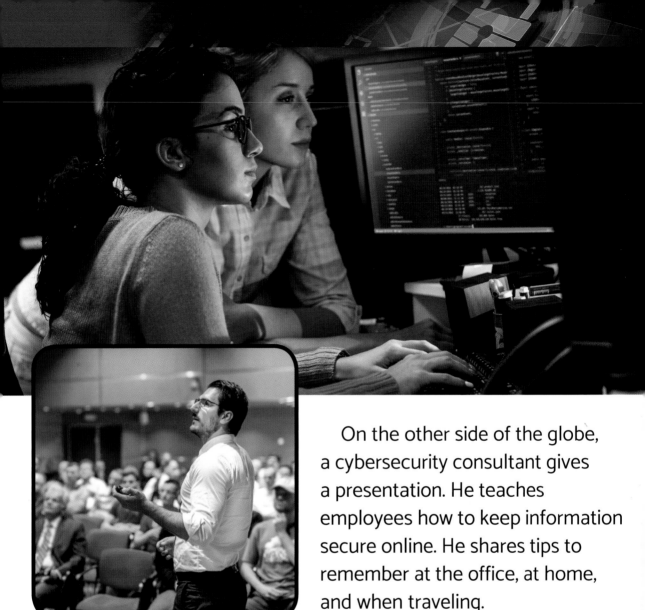

On the other side of the globe, a cybersecurity consultant gives a presentation. He teaches employees how to keep information secure online. He shares tips to remember at the office, at home, and when traveling.

Around the clock and around the world, people are working in the exciting field of cybersecurity. A STEAM education helps them do this.

STEAM Fast Fact:

STEAM stands for science, technology, engineering, art, and math. Cybersecurity involves many STEAM subjects, including computer science, information technology (IT), network engineering, psychology, forensics, and cryptography—the math and science of secret codes. Businesses and governments encourage students to explore STEAM topics so they can fill important jobs in the future.

STEAM Spotlight

Scientific subjects clearly relate to cybersecurity. How about the A in STEAM? It stands for art. Fine arts and humanities also help students prepare for cybersecurity careers. When students make musical patterns, craft visual art, and write logically, they develop creativity and design-thinking. These are critical skills for analyzing and responding to cyber-threats.

HACKING'S HIGH COSTS

Email. Texts. Television. Web browsing. For many people, the internet is integral to daily life. More than 17 billion devices are connected to it. A staggering amount of information flows through it. All of it is sent as ones and zeros—on and off pulses of electricity or light. Those ones and zeros comprise every song, photo, email, and text message ever sent. They also form every bank statement, hospital record, military plan, and personal password ever transmitted by a computer.

Cybersecurity professionals secure this digital information. They design ways to build reliable computer networks and protect them from uninvited guests.

STEAM Fast Fact:

Computers and mobile phones are not the only objects connected to cyberspace. So are new cars, smartwatches, fitness trackers, smart refrigerators, security cameras, baby monitors, printers, and many other gadgets and appliances. These devices belong to the internet of things (IoT). If users don't change the passwords that come with these devices, hackers can easily break in.

Demand for cybersecurity jobs is soaring. One reason is that hacking—breaking into computers without authorization—has become a widespread and **lucrative** crime. At least 97 percent of America's largest 500 companies and many of its small businesses have been hacked. These crimes cost people and organizations billions of dollars a year.

There is a hacker attack on an internet-connected computer every 39 seconds, according to a University of Maryland study.

Real STEAM Job:
Cybersecurity Analyst

Cybersecurity analysts help organizations defend against cyberattacks. They use knowledge of network engineering, computer science, and psychology to figure out where computer security may be weak. If hackers break in, analysts assess what happened and plan a response.

Sometimes, hackers use stolen information themselves. Other times, they profit by selling information on the underground market.

When hackers gain access to private records, it's called a *data breach*. Criminals use all sorts of stolen data to make money. With credit card numbers, they can shop online. With bank account numbers, they can withdraw funds. With medical records, they can file fake insurance claims or buy prescription drugs to sell on the black market.

Millions of records are stolen every day from data breaches, according to cybersecurity experts.

Often, hackers obtain people's personal identification information, such as their name, birthdate, address, phone number, and social security number. They use this to pretend to be someone else online—a crime called *identity theft*. They might file a **fraudulent** tax return or apply for a loan or credit card, leaving the victim with the bill. If they locate user IDs and passwords, all these crimes are easier.

Frequently changing your passwords and disconnecting your devices from the internet when not in use can help keep your information safe from hackers.

STEAM Spotlight

There were more than 250 data breaches in just six months in 2018. Fifteen of those exposed more than a million records each. The table below gives examples of a few of the large breaches that made news from 2013 to 2018.

Year	Company or Entity	Industry or Organization	Number of Records Affected or Accessible	Type of Data Released or Potentially Made Available
2018	Facebook	Social media	30 million	• Personal identification information such as name, gender, and hometown
2018	Marriott	Hotel	up to 383 million	• Personal identification information such as name, address, email, date of birth, and some passport numbers • Reservation information
2018	Cathay Pacific	Airline	9.4 million	• Personal identification information including passport numbers and government ID numbers for some accounts • Information on past travels
2018	Fortnite	Video games	estimates vary	• Personal identification information • Game accounts
2018	UnityPoint Health	Healthcare	1.4 million	• Personal identification information • Payment information for some accounts • Medical information
2018	Exactis	Marketing	340 million	• Personal identification information including addresses, phone numbers, and ages and genders of children

Year	Company or Entity	Industry or Organization	Number of Records Affected or Accessible	Type of Data Released or Potentially Made Available
2017	Equifax	Marketing	143 million	• Personal identification information including name, birthdate, social security number, and potentially address, gender, phone number, driver's license number, and email address • Some credit card numbers and tax IDs
2016	Uber	Transportation	57 million	• Personal identification information including names, phone numbers, addresses, and some driver's license numbers
2015	U.S. Office of Personnel Management	Government of United States	21.5 million	• Personal identification information including employment records and some fingerprints
2014	Home Depot	Retail store	56 million	• Personal identification information such as email addresses • Credit card data
2013	Target	Retail store	70 million customers	• Personal identification information • Payment card information
2013	Yahoo	Social media	three billion	• Personal identification information including names, birthdates, and phone numbers • Login credentials such as passwords

It's not just individuals that are at risk. Cybercriminals steal corporate trade secrets, effectively robbing companies of years of investment in research. They access government databases and may steal **personnel** records, military technologies, and battle or defense plans.

The global average cost of a data breach is 3.86 million dollars.

Corporate Espionage

To combat data breach losses, global spending on cybersecurity is expected to reach one trillion dollars by 2021.

Real STEAM Job: Cybersecurity Consultant

When organizations need additional cybersecurity expertise, sometimes they hire a consultant. Cybersecurity consultants work for different clients on a variety of projects. They test and analyze a company's systems and then recommend ways to improve security.

A TOOLKIT OF TRICKS

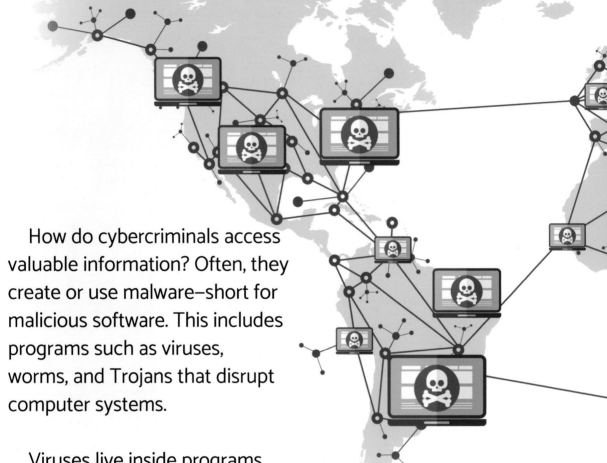

How do cybercriminals access valuable information? Often, they create or use malware–short for malicious software. This includes programs such as viruses, worms, and Trojans that disrupt computer systems.

Viruses live inside programs or files. When a person runs an infected program or file, the virus activates and spreads. People pass viruses along by sharing or emailing infected files or by connecting to unsafe websites. Worms don't need a host program, nor do they need help from humans to multiply. They search for uninfected computers in a network and spread to them on their own. Trojans enter a computer disguised as a free game or other program, but they deliver a secret attack once opened.

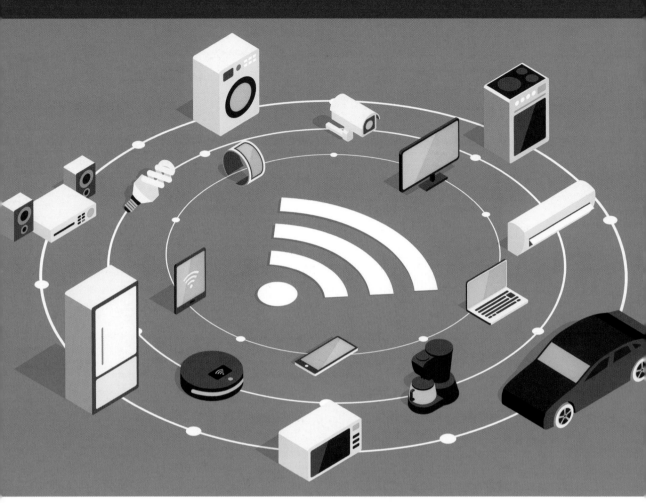

Billions of devices worldwide are connected to the internet. The devices, which make up the IoT, collect and share data.

Bots are another type of threat. They are computers or IoT devices that a hacker takes over and controls from a remote location. Owners may not even realize a hacker is using their internet connection and processing power.

One master may connect and control thousands of bots, forming a botnet or zombie army. When all the bots contact the same network, server, or application repeatedly, the botnet overwhelms it. There is more traffic in bandwidth or bytes than it can process. The result? Customers and employees can't use the flooded system. This is called a *distributed denial-of-service* or DDoS attack.

STEAM Fast Fact:

DDoS attacks have paralyzed businesses, universities, and even small countries. To carry out these attacks, hackers build huge zombie armies of IoT devices. Many owners never change the default passwords for these devices, and hackers know the passwords. They build malware to locate the devices and take them over.

Creating malware requires technical expertise. Sometimes it involves finding a backdoor—a secret entrance to a system or a means of **bypassing** security measures. But in many cases, hackers enter directly: They trick people into sharing their account numbers and login details. This is called *social engineering*. Hackers engineer a way to use social interactions to steal data from unsuspecting persons.

Real STEAM Job:
Malware Analyst

Once malware is discovered, analysts may spend weeks trying to understand its goal and structure. What is it targeting? Is it downloading data? Erasing it? How? After malware analysts figure out the program, they may write new computer code to prevent the malware from spreading and causing additional harm.

Phishing is a common form of social engineering. A hacker sends an email message that entices the reader to click on a link. The email looks like it's from a **legitimate** source, such as a boss or a bank. Users don't realize that clicking on the link activates a virus or other malware.

RANSOMWARE ATTACK

Your personal files are encrypted

You have 5 days to submit the payment!!!
To retrieve the Private key you need to pay

Your files will be lost

STEAM Fast Fact:

Criminals may disable a computer system—holding it hostage—and demand a **ransom** to fix it. A famous ransomware attack was the WannaCry worm of 2017. It infected hundreds of thousands of computers worldwide. Authorities linked the attack to a hacking group backed by the North Korean government.

Real STEAM Job: Cyber-Forensic Investigator

Figuring out the who, what, when, where, and why of cybercrime is difficult. Cyber-forensic investigators are technical sleuths who do this. Law enforcement uses their findings as evidence in court.

Audit trails in the digital world provide detailed records of all the activity that occurs on a system. By closely monitoring these trails, companies can detect possible security breaches.

DESIGNING A DEFENSE

To understand cyberdefense, it helps to know how digital information travels. All the information soaring through cyberspace travels as packets of data. Each invisible packet is a little like an envelope being sent through the mail—it includes content as well as instructions on where it's going and where it's from. When packets arrive at a **router**, the router reads these instructions and determines where to send the packets.

Packets travel the internet via wires, fiber-optic cables, and radio waves. It takes many packets to make one photo or document, and those packets may take separate routes.

As they reach their destination, the receiving device reassembles them. In what seems like no time, a photo or document completes its trip and appears on your screen.

Cybersecurity pros strengthen security along this entire path. Their work involves hardware—computers, phones, cables, routers, and servers—as well as the software that directs data through these components.

Routers are like the post offices of cyberspace, receiving data packets and routing them to their final destinations.

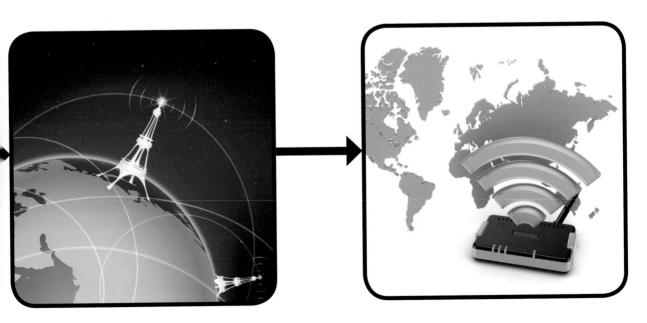

One tool they use is a firewall. Firewalls monitor traffic entering and exiting a network. Security professionals set them up to exclude data that uses particular protocols or comes from suspicious sources.

Firewalls may be hardware, software, or a combination of both. They monitor data packets to check their safety based on a set of established rules.

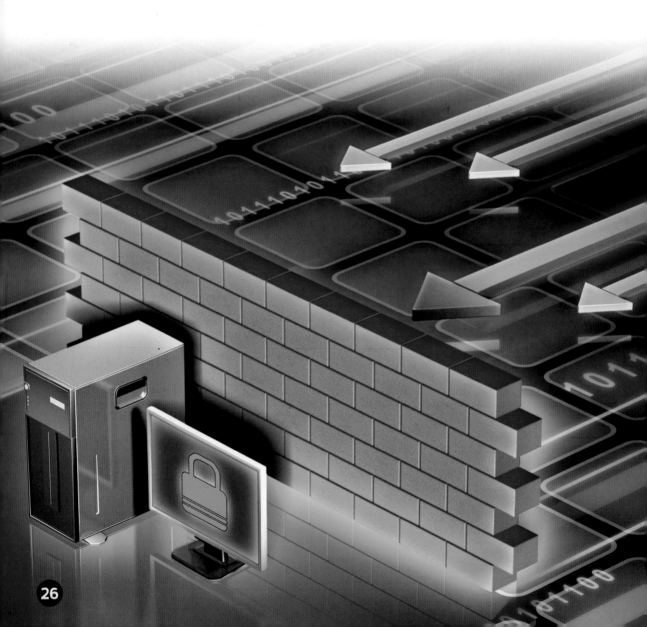

Encryption is another important security measure. It protects data by converting it into a secret code. Encrypted files can only be read by those who have the key to unlock them. Websites that use this technology often have an HTTPS (Hyper Text Transfer Protocol Secure) address and display a padlock icon.

SSL Certificate

https://v

Real STEAM Job: Security Software Developer

These computer-science experts design security software, including anti-virus programs that detect and redirect dubious activity. They create fixes—called patches—for discovered vulnerabilities. They also build security features into other software. Security software developers are familiar with programming languages such as Python, Java, C++, and operating systems such as Microsoft Windows, Apple iOS, Android, and Linux.

STEAM Fast Fact:

Many hackers comb through computer code seeking new ways to break in. When they discover new vulnerabilities, they call them *zero days*. When they use one, that's a zero-day **exploit**. Why? Because cybersecurity workers knew about it zero days—and had zero days to fix it—before hackers exploited it.

Real STEAM Job: Information Security Administrator

Security administrators keep a company's cybersecurity program running. They monitor networks, keep up-to-date on potential vulnerabilities, manage risks, and install patches. They secure databases and help control who has access to them.

Real STEAM Job: Cybersecurity Engineer or Architect

These IT professionals design secure systems using any or all of the strategies you have read about. They make sure an organization implements and tests them routinely. The highest-level security engineer or architect may have the title Chief Information Security Officer.

STEAM Fast Fact:

Don't use these passwords! Thousands of people already do, so hackers often try them: 123, 1234, 12345, 123456, 1234567, 12345678, 123456789, 1234567890, qwerty, qwertyuiop, password, password1, passw0rd, 000000, 111111, 666666, 121212, abc123, 123123, 123321, monkey, dragon, flower, sunshine, iloveyou, football, baseball, admin, letmein, login, master, welcome, hello, starwars.

STEAM Spotlight

Follow these tips to secure your devices online.

- Look for domain names that include HTTPS or SSL (Secure Sockets Layer). These use encryption.

- Install software updates. They often contain patches to correct security flaws.

- Use two-factor authentication. This adds protection by requiring more than a password to log in. Often, the second form of authentication is a code sent to a mobile phone.

- Think before you click on a link. Make sure you know the sender and can verify the link is actually from him or her. Call the sender if you're not sure.

- Avoid using public Wi-Fi in spaces like coffee shops and airports.

- Use strong passwords. These should have at least eight digits; 15 is excellent. Combine uppercase and lowercase letters, numbers, and special characters.

- Don't use your name, birthday, or pet's name as a password. Don't simply add the number one or an exclamation point to the end of a word. Try a series of words.

- Don't use the same password for more than one account.

- Change passwords whenever you think someone may have gotten yours.

WHAT COLOR IS YOUR HAT?

At some universities, when college students study cybersecurity, the first thing they discuss isn't computers. It's ethics. Ethics deals with what is right and wrong. To act ethically means to act with honor and integrity. Colleges seek to train ethical hackers, known as *white hats* in the cybersecurity world. Their purpose is to combat cybercriminals—the *black hats*.

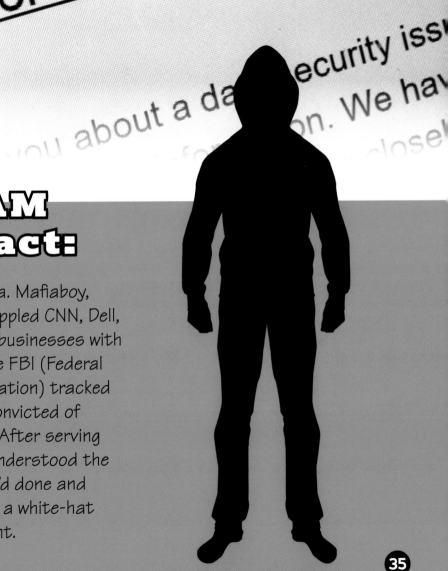

YAHOO!

NOTICE OF DATA BREACH

...you about a da... ...ecurity iss...
...on. We hav...
...closel...

STEAM Fast Fact:

Michael Calce, a.k.a. Mafiaboy, was 15 when he crippled CNN, Dell, Yahoo!, and other businesses with DDoS attacks. The FBI (Federal Bureau of Investigation) tracked him, and he was convicted of numerous crimes. After serving his sentence, he understood the impact of what he'd done and eventually became a white-hat security consultant.

Many nations have laws against hacking. For example, the United States has the Computer Fraud and Abuse Act (CFAA), which prohibits computer-related crimes including fraud, theft, **espionage**, and selling passwords.

People convicted of CFAA crimes face up to 20 years in prison in the U.S.

Real STEAM Job: Cybersecurity Lawyer

   As conflicts in cyberspace grow, so does the demand for lawyers who are tech-savvy. Governments and corporations need these professionals to develop cases against criminal hackers, who are experts at hiding their digital tracks. Clients also hire cyber-law experts to guide them as victims of identity theft and privacy breaches.

THE FUTURE IN THIS NEW FRONTIER

One of the scariest aspects of cybersecurity involves the possibility of cyber-war. In a cyber-war scenario, nations would use computer attacks to cause physical harm, destruction, or loss of life. Since many aspects of modern life depend on computers, this kind of attack could take many forms. What if water treatment plants stopped disinfecting a city's water? Or electricity plants could not power homes and hospitals? Or air traffic control networks were shut down? If foreign hackers sabotaged these systems, the results could be tragic.

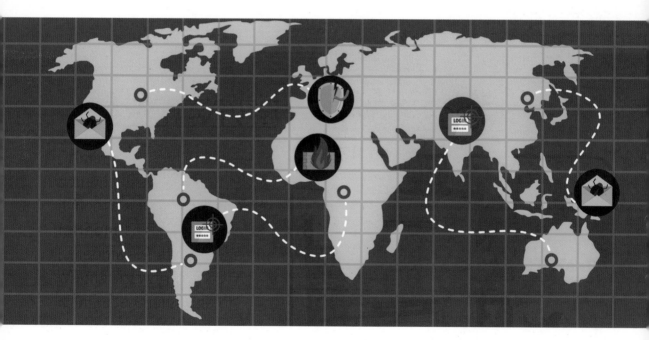

In response to these threats, nations have created cybersecurity defense units. The United States has them within the Department of Homeland Security and the National Security Agency (NSA).

STEAM Fast Fact:

In 2009, machinery at an Iranian nuclear facility began to malfunction. The cause? An extremely complex computer worm dubbed Stuxnet. Though no one has claimed responsibility, many think the United States and Israel created Stuxnet. These nations suspected Iran was enriching uranium for use in nuclear weapons, violating a treaty.

Because the facility was not connected to the internet, it is suspected that someone used a removable USB drive to infect the system.

STEAM Fast Fact:

The United States National Security Agency (NSA) funds free GenCyber camps in almost every state. These camps introduce students to all sorts of cybersecurity projects—from phishing to forensics. There are camps for middle school students and high school students. Check online to learn about these opportunities.

Cybersecurity is "at the top of the list" of technical needs and challenges the world faces, according to Joel Rasmus of Purdue University. But people and nations—including China, Russia, and the United States—disagree on how best to maintain security in the cyber realm.

What happens when a person's desire for privacy conflicts with a nation's desire for gathering information? Should nations regulate the internet within their borders, potentially limiting what is on it? Should spying on other nations be permitted? Should governments interfere in other nations' elections?

STEAM Spotlight

Joel Rasmus, Managing Director of the Center for Education and Research in Information Assurance and Security (CERIAS) at Purdue University, shares his thoughts on cybersecurity and the skills students need to work in this field.

Is cybersecurity currently improving?

"Yes, we are absolutely getting better at this. But the problem is dramatically growing. Every day there are millions—literally millions—of new endpoints coming online, and every one of them is a potential vulnerability or risk or attack-vector."

Even if they do not tamper with vote counts, should they spread information with the goal of influencing voters? If they do, how should a nation respond? Cybersecurity professionals of the future will tackle the technical and ethical issues these questions raise.

What education should students pursue for a career in cybersecurity?

"There are traditional paths to cybersecurity like studying computer engineering or computer science or applied technologies. But there are many other avenues. The underlying theme is that people going into this field should be problem-solvers. It's an extremely creative industry. There are all kinds of examples of people who have degrees like creative writing or art history who are doing very well in this industry.

"Diversity is hugely important...diversity of cultures, diversity of gender, diversity of thought. We need people who can look at problems in a creative way from a variety of perspectives."

STEAM JOB FACTS

Cyber-Incident Responder

Important Skills: keeping calm in a crisis, thinking quickly, ability to work alone and in groups, problem-solving, attention to detail

Important Knowledge: computer networking, programming, cybersecurity methods

College Major: computer information technology, cybersecurity, computer science

Penetration (Pen) Tester

Important Skills: ability to work independently, verbal and written communication, time-management, commitment to ethical behavior, critical reasoning, coding

Important Knowledge: hardware and network systems, computer languages such as Python and Java, operating systems such as Unix and Linux

College Major: computer science, computer information technology, or a degree related to business or communications along with coursework in computer subjects

Cybersecurity Analyst or Engineer

Important Skills: analytical thinking, creative thinking, computer programming, problem-solving, attention to detail

Important Knowledge: network architecture, operating systems, cybersecurity practices, psychology, forensics, database design

College Major: cybersecurity, computer science, computer and information technology, computer engineering, or a degree in the humanities such as philosophy, English, or arts along with coursework in computer subjects and information technology (IT)

Security Software Developer

Important Skills: computer programming, creative thinking, problem-solving, logic, ability to work with teams

Important Knowledge: computer languages, applications, network solutions

College Major: computer science, computer engineering, math, computer technology

Cryptographer

Important Skills: math, logic, analytical thinking, critical reasoning, pattern recognition

Important Knowledge: binary computer code, computer languages, computer programs, statistics

College Major: math, computer science, computer engineering

Cybersecurity Lawyer

Important Skills: critical thinking, reading comprehension, writing, verbal communication

Important Knowledge: cybersecurity law and policy, computer networking, information technology, ethics

College Major: English, history, philosophy, computer science, math, or cybersecurity, followed by a law degree

GLOSSARY

bypassing (BYE-pas-ing): avoiding something by using a different route

encryption (in-KRIP-shuhn): a method of writing in secret code; a process for making digital information unreadable except to those who have the key to translate it

espionage (ES-pee-uh-nahzh): the act of spying, or the work of a spy for a government or organization

exploit (EK-sploit): a brave or exciting action, or in the computer field, a cyber-threat that takes advantage of a weakness or flaw

fraudulent (FRAWD-juh-luhnt): dishonest; intended to deceive people or get money from them

legitimate (luh-JIT-uh-mit): in keeping with the law or rules; reasonable or justified

lucrative (LOO-kruh-tiv): producing wealth; profitable

personnel (pur-suh-NEL): related to the group of people who work for a company or an organization

ransom (RAN-suhm): money that is demanded before someone (or something) being held captive can be set free

router (ROU-tur): a device that handles signals between computers or computer networks

INDEX

TEXT-DEPENDENT QUESTIONS

1. How can studying the arts help a person pursue a career in cybersecurity?
2. What is identity theft?
3. Have any data breaches affected more than a billion records?
4. What are three different types of malware?
5. What are some tools and activities that cybersecurity professionals use to help protect digital data?

EXTENSION ACTIVITY

Make a poster or video to teach your family about cybersecurity. Include a section on making strong passwords. Include another section on identifying and deleting phishing emails. Remind people NOT to click on links that seem suspicious or that come from people they don't know. Add sections about identifying secure websites and protecting personal information. What other information can you share? With your help, your family will be safer online.

ABOUT THE AUTHOR

Cynthia Argentine writes books, poems, and magazine articles for children of all ages. She lives in the Midwest with her husband and three children. When she's not researching or writing, she is likely playing piano, taking a walk with her dog, or planning travels and adventures with her family. In college, she studied English, environmental science, and environmental law. She thinks a STEAM job in cybersecurity sounds fascinating.

www.rourkeeducationalmedia.com

PHOTO CREDITS: Cover: main photo © LeoWolfert, padlock image © vs148; Pages 4-5 Office workers at night © Rawpixel.com, presentation © Matej Kastelic, when at computer© Solis Images; Pages 6-7 girl artist © RossHelen, musicians © Golubovy, globe with code image © Ase; Page 8 © Panchenko Vladimir, Page 9 hacker © Artem Oleshko, woman at computers © Andrey_Popov; Pages 10-11 green screen © Michael H Jones, woman at computer © PR Image Factory, laptop © zimmytws, illustration © Inspiring, man with bill © fizkes; Pages 14-15 Corporate Espionage image © Stuart Miles, computers with maps © Gorodenkoff; Pages 16-17 World Map © MaDedee, man © Phovoir, Page 18 IoT devices © Graf Vishenka, Page 19 DDOS ATTACK image © FrameStockFootages, user/password image © frank_peters; Pages 20-21 Programmer © Dragon Images, magnifying glass © Stefano Garau, woman at computer © Rawpixel.com; illustration © Tashal; Pages 22-23 laptop © rawf8, woman © PR Image Factory, "Investigate" image © Den Rise , map © Jaiz Anuar; Pages 24-25 laptop © Billion Photos, satellite dish © improvize, abstract image © improvize, globe © Vectomart; router and map © 3Dstock, router in home © Casezy idea; Page 26 firewall © Andrea Danti, Page 27 using laptop © TippaPatt , HTTPS padlock © Marc Bruxelle; Page 28 © Gorodenkoff, Page 29 zero day exploit © Stephen Finn, man coding © Ollyy; Page 30 Information Security Administrator © Gorodenkoff, Page 31 hacked © Vladnik, written passwords © designer491; Page 32 SSL image © Sashkin, computer update image © vectorplus, Page 33 verification code image © Aa Amie, passwords © designer491; Pages 34-35 college class © Gorodenkoff, illustrations black ha white hat © MatiasDelCarmine, Yahoo notice Editorial credit: dennizn / Shutterstock.com, black figure © Serhii Borodin; Page 36 © eakasarn, Page 37 © YP_Studio; Page 38 © Anatolir, Page 39 © Photographee.eu; Page 40 © Rido, page 41 © Gwoeii All images from Shutterstock.com except: Page 40 National Security Agency logo courtesy of U.S. Government and diagrams © Grixlkraxl https://creativecommons.org/licenses/©-sa/3.0/deed.en

Edited by: Kim Thompson
Produced by Blue Door Education for Rourke Educational Media. Cover and interior design by: Nicola Stratford

Library of Congress PCN Data

STEAM Jobs in Cybersecurity / Cynthia Argentine
(STEAM Jobs You'll Love)
 ISBN 978-1-73161-480-3 (hard cover)
 ISBN 978-1-73161-287-8 (soft cover)
 ISBN 978-1-73161-585-5 (e-Book)
 ISBN 978-1-73161-690-6 (e-Pub)
Library of Congress Control Number: 2019932459

Rourke Educational Media
Printed in the United States of America,
North Mankato, Minnesota